Journey 2 Victory

A Daily Journal to Your Spiritual Victory

Chuck & Mae Dettman

Copyright 2016 Chuck and Mae Dettman

All rights reserved.

ISBN-10: 0-9838987-9-0

ISBN-13: 978-0-9838987-9-5

Second Printing

This publication is intended to provide accurate information regarding the subject matter covered. It is sold with the understanding that neither the authors nor the publisher are engaged in rendering psychological, financial or other professional services. If professional assistance or counseling is needed, the services of a competent professional should be sought.

Referencing of materials in this book is not meant to imply any endorsement of the author, publisher, or organization that created those materials.

Copyright © 2016 Chuck and Mae Dettman. All rights reserved.

No part of this publication may be reproduced, stored in a retrieval system, or transmitted in any form or by any means— electronic, mechanical, photocopying, recording, or otherwise— without the prior written permission of the authors. The only exception is brief quotations in printed reviews.

Unless otherwise noted, all scripture verses used are from Holy Bible, New International Version®, NIV® Copyright ©1973, 1978, 1984, 2011 by Biblica, Inc.® Used by permission. All rights reserved worldwide.

ISBN 13: 978-0-9838987-9-5

ISBN 10: 0-9838987-9-0

1. Devotions aspects-Christianity. 2. Marriage-Biblical teaching. 3. Relationships. 4. Interpersonal relations–Religious aspects–Christianity. 5. Journaling

This book is available at large quantity discounts for use in denominational or regional marriage initiatives and can be customized with your organization or denomination's logo. For more information, contact Sales@TheMarriage-Journey.com.

This book is available in print at most online retailers.

Introduction

Journey 2 Victory serves as a tool to assist in healing not only marriages and relationships, but also individuals. Many times when our thoughts are committed to paper God gives us comfort and 'releases' our hurt and pain.

This is a journal designed to give you a sense of freedom and peace using a word, with a related scripture verse, to reflect and pray your struggles to Him. Each day select a word that is significant, pray the scripture for that word and then journal your thoughts.

Once you've completed the journal (journey) for the word use that scripture to help guide you through your day. You might feel comfortable sharing your thoughts with a friend, family member, your pastor or spouse. Most important, let God 'speak' to you imparting His Will for the day.

Another use for the ***Journey 2 Victory*** is to supplement the Navigational Cards found in ***The Marriage Journey: A flight Plan to Your Healthy Marriage.*** The cards are a simple tool to assist in conversations at home, school, work or just about anywhere. Check them out at http://themarriage-journey.com/navigation-card-purchase.html.
Instructions are on the site as well, or you'll find them in Chapter 18 for *The Marriage Journey.*

Inspirational Words

Introduction	iv
Inspirational Words	5
Abilities	15
Accomplishment	16
Acknowledge	17
Action	18
Adequate	19
Advantage	20
Adversity	21
Advice	22
Affecting	23
Agape Love	24
Aging	25
Alignment	26
Alliance	27
Ambition	28
Anger	29
Anoint	30
Answer	31
Anticipation	32
Anxiety	33
Apathy	34
Apology	35
Appreciate	36
Approval	37
Art	38
Articulate	39
Aspire	40
Association	41
Assumptions	42
Assurance	43
Attitude	44
Authenticity	45

Authority	46
Available	47
Avoidance	48
Backsliding	49
Balance	50
Barriers	51
Beginnings	52
Behavior	53
Beliefs	54
Benefactor	55
Benefit	56
Birth	57
Blessings	58
Blooming	59
Boldness	60
Boredom	61
Boundaries	62
Branding	63
Bravery	64
Building	65
Business	66
Busyness	67
Camaraderie	68
Carelessness	69
Caring	70
Caution	71
Celebrate	72
Centered	73
Challenges	74
Champions	75
Change	76
Character	77
Charity	78
Choices	79
Circumstances	80
Clarity	81
Coachable	82
Cohabitation	83

Collaboration	84
Comfort	85
Commitment	86
Communication	87
Compassion	88
Competition	89
Complacency	90
Compliant	91
Compromise	92
Condemnation	93
Confession	94
Confidence	95
Conflict	96
Connected	97
Conscience	98
Consequences	99
Consideration	100
Consistency	101
Contentment	102
Continuation	103
Control	104
Conviction	105
Courage	106
Creation	107
Crisis	108
Critical	109
Culture	110
Curiosity	111
Death	112
Decision	113
Deliverance	114
Desires	115
Destination	116
Diligence	117
Discernment	118
Discipleship	119
Discourage	120
Discover	121

Disposition **122**
Distribution **123**
Doubt **124**
Dream **125**
Dryness **126**
Duty **127**
Dynamic **128**
Edge **129**
Edify **130**
Efficiency **131**
Effort **132**
Ego **133**
Emerging **134**
Emotions **135**
Empowered **136**
Emptiness **137**
Encourage **138**
Encouragement **139**
Endurance **140**
Enemies **141**
Enrich **142**
Envision **143**
Evolve **144**
Example **145**
Excuses **146**
Execute **147**
Expectation **148**
Experience **149**
Failure **150**
Fairness **151**
Faith **152**
Faithfulness **153**
Family **154**
Fantastic **155**
Fatigue **156**
Favor **157**
Flexibility **158**
Finding **159**

Finishing	160
Focus	161
Foolish	162
Forgiveness	163
Freedom	164
Friendship	165
Frustration	166
Fun	167
Fundamentals	168
Future	169
Generations	170
Generosity	171
Gentleness	172
Gifts	173
Give Up	174
Goal	175
Good-bye	176
Goodness	177
Grace	178
Gratitude	179
Greatness	180
Grief	181
Guard Your Heart	182
Guidance	183
Guilt	184
Gumption	185
Habits	186
Happiness	187
Hard work	188
Harmony	189
Healing	190
Healthy	191
Heaven	192
Heritage	193
Holiness	194
Honor	195
Hope	196
Humility	197

Humor	198
Hungry	199
Idolatry	200
Ignite	201
Imagination	202
Impact	203
Impatient	204
Incredible	205
Independence	206
Injustice	207
Insight	208
Integrity	209
Intentional	210
Intimacy	211
Intuition	212
Investment	213
Joy	214
Justice	215
Kindness	216
Leadership	217
Learn	218
Liaison	219
Lighthouse	220
Limitations	221
Listening	222
Loneliness	223
Love	224
Loyalty	225
Maintenance	226
Manners	227
Mastering	228
Maturity	229
Maximum	230
Meaning	231
Mentorship	232
Mercy	233
Method	234
Ministry	235

Miracles	236
Mistakes	237
Money	238
Motivation	239
Motives	240
Multiplication	241
Naïve	242
Nation	243
Needs	244
Neighbor	245
Nurture	246
Obedient	247
Obligation	248
Obstacle	249
Opportunity	250
Opposition	251
Optimism	252
Options	253
Order	254
Overcome	255
Overwhelmed	256
Pain	257
Paradigm	258
Partnership	259
Past	260
Patience	261
Perception	262
Perfect	263
Personality	264
Perspective	265
Pleasure	266
Plunge	267
Poise	268
Positivity	269
Potential	270
Power	271
Prayer	272
Precious	273

Prepare	274
Present	275
Pressure	276
Pride	277
Productivity	278
Professional	279
Projection	280
Promise	281
Prompt	282
Purity	283
Purpose	284
Pursue	285
Quality	286
Quitting	287
Reconciliation	288
Reflect	289
Rejection	290
Relationship	291
Relevance	292
Remarriage	293
Renewal	294
Reputation	295
Resist	296
Resolution	297
Respect	298
Responsibility	299
Rest	300
Restlessness	301
Restore	302
Result	303
Retention	304
Revenge	305
Risk	306
Roles	307
Romance	308
Sacrifice	309
Salvation	310
Sanity	311

Satisfaction	312
Schedule	313
Scope	314
Security	315
Seduction	316
Servant	317
Sharing	318
Simple	319
Skeptic	320
Solitude	321
Sorrow	322
Stability	323
Status	324
Steadfast	325
Storm	326
Strength	327
Stress	328
Stretch	329
Strive	330
Stubborn	331
Success	332
Support	333
Surrender	334
Symbol	335
System	336
Tactical	337
Talent	338
Teach	339
Teamwork	340
Temptation	341
Testing	342
Therapeutic	343
Think	344
Thoughts	345
Time	346
Timing	347
Tithing	348
Today	349

Training	350
Transgressions	351
Tranquility	352
Transformation	353
Transparent	354
Travel	355
Treasure	356
Trend	357
Trouble	358
Trust	359
Trustworthy	360
Truth	361
Understanding	362
Unwavering	363
Used	364
Value	365
Victory	366
Vision	367
Voice	368
Vulnerability	369
Warrior	370
Weakness	371
Wealth	372
Winner	373
Witness	374
Words	375
Work	376
Worry	377
Worship	378
Zeal	379
About the Authors	381
Other Works by Chuck & Mae	383
Connect with Us	387

Journey 2 Victory

Abilities

Romans 12:6-8

We have different gifts, according to the grace given to each of us. If your gift is prophesying, then prophesy in accordance with your faith; if it is serving, then serve; if it is teaching, then teach; if it is to encourage, then give encouragement; if it is giving, then give generously; if it is to lead, do it diligently; if it is to show mercy, do it cheerfully.

Accomplishment

John 15:16

You did not choose me, but I chose you and appointed you so that you might go and bear fruit—fruit that will last—and so that whatever you ask in my name the Father will give you.

Acknowledge

Matthew 10:32

Whoever acknowledges me before others, I will also acknowledge before my Father in heaven.

Action

1 Peter 2:1-3

Therefore, rid yourselves of all malice and all deceit, hypocrisy, envy, and slander of every kind. Like newborn babies, crave pure spiritual milk, so that by it you may grow up in your salvation, now that you have tasted that the Lord is good.

Journey 2 Victory

Adequate

1 Timothy 5:8

Anyone who does not provide for their relatives, and especially for their own household, has denied the faith and is worse than an unbeliever.

Advantage

1 Thessalonians 4:6

And that in this matter no one should wrong or take advantage of a brother or sister The Lord will punish all those who commit such sins, as we told you and warned you before.

Journey 2 Victory

Adversity

Proverbs 17:17

A friend loves at all times, and a brother is born for a time of adversity.

Journey 2 Victory

Advice

Proverbs 19:20

Listen to advice and accept discipline, and at the end you will be counted among the wise.

Journey 2 Victory

Affecting

Proverbs 13:20

Walk with the wise and become wise, for a companion of fools suffers harm.

Journey 2 Victory

Agape Love

1 John 4:8

Whoever does not love does not know God, because God is love.

Journey 2 Victory

Aging

Psalm 71:18

Even when I am old and gray, do not forsake me, my God, till I declare your power to the next generation, your mighty acts to all who are to come.

Journey 2 Victory

Alignment

Genesis 6:2

The sons of God saw that the daughters of humans were beautiful, and they married any of them they chose.

Journey 2 Victory

Alliance

Galatians 3:28

There is neither Jew nor Gentile, neither slave nor free, nor is there male and female, for you are all one in Christ Jesus.

Ambition

Luke 9:25

What good is it for someone to gain the whole world, and yet lose or forfeit their very self?

Journey 2 Victory

Anger

Proverbs 29:11

Fools give full vent to their rage, but the wise bring calm in the end.

Journey 2 Victory

Anoint

2 Timothy 2:15

Do your best to present yourself to God as one approved, a worker who does not need to be ashamed and who correctly handles the word of truth.

った
Answer

1 Peter 3:15

But in your hearts revere Christ as Lord. Always be prepared to give an answer to everyone who asks you to give the reason for the hope that you have. But do this with gentleness and respect,

Journey 2 Victory

Anticipation

Acts 1:11

"Men of Galilee," they said, "why do you stand here looking into the sky? This same Jesus, who has been taken from you into heaven, will come back in the same way you have seen him go into heaven."

Journey 2 Victory

Anxiety

1Peter 5:6-7

Humble yourselves, therefore, under the mighty hand of God so that at the proper time he may exalt you, casting all your anxieties on him, because he cares for you.

Apathy

Proverbs 15:19

The way of the sluggard is blocked with thorns, but the path of the upright is a highway.

Journey 2 Victory

Apology

Acts 4:12

Salvation is found in no one else, for there is no other name under heaven given to mankind by which we must be saved.

Journey 2 Victory

Appreciate

Hebrews 13:4

Marriage should be honored by all, and the marriage bed kept pure, for God will judge the adulterer and all the sexually immoral.

Journey 2 Victory

Approval

Galatians 1:10

Am I now trying to win the approval of human beings, or of God? Or am I trying to please people? If I were still trying to please people, I would not be a servant of Christ.

Art

Revelation 21:11

It shone with the glory of God, and its brilliance was like that of a very precious jewel, like jasper, clear as crystal.

Journey 2 Victory

Articulate

Romans 10:17

Consequently, faith comes from hearing the message, and the message is heard through the word about Christ.

Journey 2 Victory

Aspire

1 Timothy 1:5

The goal of this command is love, which comes from a pure heart and a good conscience and a sincere faith.

Journey 2 Victory

Association

Colossians 1:16

For in him all things were created: things in heaven and on earth, visible and invisible, whether thrones or powers or rulers or authorities; all things have been created through him and for him.

Assumptions

1 Corinthians 4:5

Therefore judge nothing before the appointed time; wait until the Lord comes. He will bring to light what is hidden in darkness and will expose the motives of the heart. At that time each will receive their praise from God.

Journey 2 Victory

Assurance

Hebrews 12:28

Therefore, since we are receiving a kingdom that cannot be shaken, let us be thankful, and so worship God acceptably with reverence and awe,

Attitude

Philippians 2:14-15

Do everything without grumbling or arguing, so that you may become blameless and pure, "children of God without fault in a warped and crooked generation." Then you will shine among them like stars in the sky.

Journey 2 Victory

Authenticity

2 Timothy 3:16

"All Scripture is God-breathed and is useful for teaching, rebuking, correcting and training in righteousness,"

Journey 2 Victory

Authority

Romans 13:1

Let everyone be subject to the governing authorities, for there is no authority except that which God has established. God has established the authorities that exist.

Journey 2 Victory

Available

1 Thessalonians 5:24

The one who calls you is faithful, and he will do it.

Avoidance

Romans 16:17

I urge you, brothers and sisters, to watch out for those who cause divisions and put obstacles in your way that are contrary to the teaching you have learned. Keep away from them.

Journey 2 Victory

Backsliding

Jeremiah 14:7

Although our sins testify against us, do something, LORD, for the sake of your name. For we have often rebelled; we have sinned against you.

Balance

Proverbs 16:11

*Honest scales and balances belong to the L*ORD*; all the weights in the bag are of his making.*

Journey 2 Victory

Barriers

Galatians 5:19-21

Now the works of the flesh are evident: sexual immorality, impurity, sensuality, idolatry, sorcery, enmity, strife, jealousy, fits of anger, rivalries, dissensions, divisions, envy drunkenness, orgies, and things like these. I warn you, as I warned you before, that those who do such things will not inherit the kingdom of God.

Journey 2 Victory

Beginnings

2 Corinthians 5:17

Therefore, if anyone is in Christ, the new creation has come. The old has gone, the new is here!

Behavior

Hebrews 10:26

If we deliberately keep on sinning after we have received the knowledge of the truth, no sacrifice for sins is left.

Journey 2 Victory

Beliefs

1 Corinthians 6:19

Do you not know that your bodies are temples of the Holy Spirit, who is in you, whom you have received from God? You are not your own;

Journey 2 Victory

Benefactor

Deuteronomy 18:15

The L<small>ORD</small> your God will raise up for you a prophet like me from among you, from your fellow Israelites. You must listen to him.

Benefit

1 Timothy 5:8

Anyone who does not provide for their relatives, and especially for their own household, has denied the faith and is worse than an unbeliever.

Journey 2 Victory

Birth

Jeremiah 1:5

Before I formed you in the womb I knew you, before you were born I set you apart; I appointed you as a prophet to the nations.

Blessings

Psalm 84:11

For the LORD God is a sun and shield; the LORD bestows favor and honor; no good thing does he withhold from those whose walk is blameless.

Blooming

Colossians 3:1-2

Since, then, you have been raised with Christ, set your hearts on things above, where Christ is, seated at the right hand of God. Set your minds on things above, not on earthly things.

Boldness

2 Corinthians 7:4

I have spoken to you with great frankness; I take great pride in you. I am greatly encouraged; in all our troubles my joy knows no bounds.

Journey 2 Victory

Boredom

Genesis 1:28

God blessed them and said to them, "Be fruitful and increase in number; fill the earth and subdue it. Rule over the fish in the sea and the birds in the sky and over every living creature that moves on the ground."

Boundaries

Acts 17:26

From one man he made all the nations, that they should inhabit the whole earth; and he marked out their appointed times in history and the boundaries of their lands.

Journey 2 Victory

Branding

1 Timothy 2:5

For there is one God and one mediator between God and mankind, the man Christ Jesus.

Journey 2 Victory

Bravery

2 Timothy 1:7

For the Spirit God gave us does not make us timid, but gives us power, love and self-discipline.

Journey 2 Victory

Building

1 Thessalonians 5:11

Therefore encourage one another and build each other up, just as in fact you are doing.

Business

Colossians 3:17

And whatever you do, whether in word or deed, do it all in the name of the Lord Jesus, giving thanks to God the Father through him.

Journey 2 Victory

Busyness

Ephesians 5:15-17

Be very careful, then, how you live—not as unwise but as wise, making the most of every opportunity, because the days are evil. Therefore do not be foolish, but understand what the Lord's will is.

Journey 2 Victory

Camaraderie

Galatians 2:20

I have been crucified with Christ and I no longer live, but Christ lives in me. The life I now live in the body, I live by faith in the Son of God, who loved me and gave himself for me.

Carelessness

Matthew 6:24

No one can serve two masters. Either you will hate the one and love the other, or you will be devoted to the one and despise the other. You cannot serve both God and money.

Journey 2 Victory

Caring

John 13:34-35

"A new command I give you: Love one another. As I have loved you, so you must love one another. By this everyone will know that you are my disciples, if you love one another."

Journey 2 Victory

Caution

1 Thessalonians 5:21

But test them all; hold on to what is good.

Celebrate

Psalm 150:1-6

Praise the LORD.

Praise God in his sanctuary; praise him in his mighty heavens. Praise him for his acts of power; praise him for his surpassing greatness. Praise him with the sounding of the trumpet, praise him with the harp and lyre, praise him with timbrel and dancing, praise him with the strings and pipe, praise him with the clash of cymbals, praise him with resounding cymbals.
Let everything that has breath praise the LORD. Praise the LORD.

Centered

1 Corinthians 10:13

No temptation has overtaken you except what is common to mankind. And God is faithful; he will not let you be tempted beyond what you can bear. But when you are tempted he will also provide a way out so that you can endure it.

Journey 2 Victory

Challenges

James 1:2-4

Consider it pure joy, my brothers and sisters, whenever you face trials of many kinds, because you know that the testing of your faith produces perseverance. Let perseverance finish its work so that you may be mature and complete, not lacking anything.

Journey 2 Victory

Champions

Isaiah 44:24

"This is what the LORD says—your Redeemer, who formed you in the womb:

I am the LORD, the Maker of all things, who stretches out the heavens, who spreads out the earth by myself,"

Journey 2 Victory

Change

2 Corinthians 5:17

Therefore, if anyone is in Christ, the new creation has come: The old has gone, the new is here!

Character

1 Samuel 16:7

But the LORD said to Samuel, "Do not consider his appearance or his height, for I have rejected him. The LORD does not look at the things people look at. People look at the outward appearance, but the LORD looks at the heart."

Charity

Act 20:35

In everything I did, I showed you that by this kind of hard work we must help the weak, remembering the words the Lord Jesus himself said: 'It is more blessed to give than to receive.'

Journey 2 Victory

Choices

Romans 8:7

The mind governed by the flesh is hostile to God; it does not submit to God's can it do so.

Circumstances

Romans 12:19

Do not take revenge, my dear friends, but leave room for God's wrath, for it is written: "It is mine to avenge; I will repay," says the Lord.

Journey 2 Victory

Clarity

Psalm 19:7

The law of the LORD is perfect, refreshing the soul. The statutes of the LORD are trustworthy, making wise the simple.

Coachable

Romans 12:2

Do not conform to the pattern of this world, but be transformed by the renewing of your mind. Then you will be able to test and approve what God's will is—his good, pleasing and perfect will.

Journey 2 Victory

Cohabitation

Hebrews 13:4

Marriage should be honored by all, and the marriage bed kept pure, for God will judge the adulterer and all the sexually immoral.

Collaboration

Romans 12:4-6

For just as each of us has one body with many members, and these members do not all have the same function, so in Christ we, though many, form one body, and each member belongs to all the others. We have different gifts, according to the grace given to each of us. If your gift is prophesying, then prophesy in accordance with your faith.

Journey 2 Victory

Comfort

2 Corinthians 1:3-4

Praise be to the God and Father of our Lord Jesus Christ, the Father of compassion and the God of all comfort, who comforts us in all our troubles, so that we can comfort those in any trouble with the comfort we ourselves receive from God.

Journey 2 Victory

Commitment

Numbers 30:2

When a man makes a vow to the L<small>ORD</small> or takes an oath to obligate himself by a pledge, he must not break his word but must do everything he said.

Journey 2 Victory

Communication

Ephesians 4:29

Do not let any unwholesome talk come out of your mouths, but only what is helpful for building others up according to their needs, that it may benefit those who listen.

Compassion

Colossians 3:12-13

Therefore, as God's chosen people, holy and dearly loved, clothe yourselves with compassion, kindness, humility, gentleness and patience. Bear with each other and forgive one another if any of you has a grievance against someone. Forgive as the Lord forgave you.

Journey 2 Victory

Competition

2 Timothy 2:5

Similarly, anyone who competes as an athlete does not receive the victor's crown except by competing according to the rules.

Journey 2 Victory

Complacency

Revelation 3:15-16

I know your deeds, that you are neither cold nor hot. I wish you were either one or the other! So, because you are lukewarm—neither hot nor cold—I am about to spit you out of my mouth.

Journey 2 Victory

Compliant

1 Peter 3:15

But in your hearts revere Christ as Lord. Always be prepared to give an answer to everyone who asks you to give the reason for the hope that you have. But do this with gentleness and respect,

Journey 2 Victory

Compromise

Proverbs 25:28

Like a city whose walls are broken through is a person who lacks self-control.

Journey 2 Victory

Condemnation

1 John 3:20

If our hearts condemn us, we know that God is greater than our hearts, and he knows everything.

Confession

Proverbs 28:13

Whoever conceals their sins does not prosper, but the one who confesses and renounces them finds mercy.

Journey 2 Victory

Confidence

Hebrews 10:35-36

So do not throw away your confidence; it will be richly rewarded.

You need to persevere so that when you have done the will of God, you will receive what he has promised.

Conflict

Matthew 18:15-17

"If your brother or sister sins go and point out their fault, just between the two of you. If they listen to you, you have won them over. But if they will not listen, take one or two others along, so that 'every matter may be established by the testimony of two or three witnesses.' If they still refuse to listen, tell it to the church; and if they refuse to listen even to the church, treat them as you would a pagan or a tax collector."

Connected

Genesis 2:24

That is why a man leaves his father and mother and is united to his wife, and they become one flesh.

Conscience

Romans 2:15

They show that the requirements of the law are written on their hearts, their consciences also bearing witness, and their thoughts sometimes accusing them and at other times even defending them.

Journey 2 Victory

Consequences

Galatians 6:7-8

Do not be deceived: God cannot be mocked. A man reaps what he sows. Whoever sows to please their flesh, from the flesh will reap destruction; whoever sows to please the Spirit, from the Spirit will reap eternal life.

Journey 2 Victory

Consideration

Deuteronomy 32:7

Remember the days of old; consider the generations long past. Ask your father and he will tell you, your elders, and they will explain to you.

Journey 2 Victory

Consistency

Revelation 3:15-16

I know your deeds, that you are neither cold nor hot. I wish you were either one or the other! So, because you are lukewarm—neither hot nor cold—I am about to spit you out of my mouth.

Journey 2 Victory

Contentment

Hebrews 13:5

Keep your lives free from the love of money and be content with what you have, because God has said,

"Never will I leave you; never will I forsake you."

Journey 2 Victory

Continuation

Hebrews 9:27

Just as people are destined to die once, and after that to face judgment,

Journey 2 Victory

Control

2 Timothy 1:7

For the Spirit God gave us does not make us timid, but gives us power, love and self-discipline.

Journey 2 Victory

Conviction

2 Corinthians 7:9-10

Yet now I am happy, not because you were made sorry, but because your sorrow led you to repentance. For you became sorrowful as God intended and so were not harmed in any way by us. Godly sorrow brings repentance that leads to salvation and leaves no regret, but worldly sorrow brings death.

Courage

1 Chronicles 28:20

David also said to Solomon his son, "Be strong and courageous, and do the work. Do not be afraid or discouraged, for the LORD God, my God is with you. He will not fail you or forsake you until all the work for the service of the temple of the LORD is finished."

Journey 2 Victory

Creation

Colossians 1:16

For in him all things were created: things in heaven and on earth, visible and invisible, whether thrones or powers or rulers or authorities; all things have been created through him and for him.

Journey 2 Victory

Crisis

James 4:1-2

What causes fights and quarrels among you? Don't they come from your desires that battle within you? You desire but do not have, so you kill. You covet but you cannot get what you want, so you quarrel and fight. You do not have because you do not ask God.

Journey 2 Victory

Critical

James 4:11-12

Brothers and sisters do not slander one another. Anyone who speaks against a brother or sister or judges them speaks against the law and judges it. When you judge the law, you are not keeping it, but sitting in judgment on it. There is only one Lawgiver and Judge, the one who is able to save and destroy. But you—who are you to judge your neighbor?

Culture

John 15:19

If you belonged to the world, it would love you as its own. As it is, you do not belong to the world, but I have chosen you out of the world. That is why the world hates you.

Journey 2 Victory

Curiosity

John 1:5

The light shines in the darkness, and the darkness has not overcome it.

Journey 2 Victory

Death

Romans 8:10

But if Christ is in you, then even though your body is subject to death because of sin, the Spirit gives life because of righteousness.

Journey 2 Victory

Decision

Acts 2:38

Peter replied, "Repent and be baptized, every one of you, in the name of Jesus Christ for the forgiveness of your sins. And you will receive the gift of the Holy Spirit."

Journey 2 Victory

Deliverance

Exodus 14:13-14

Moses answered the people, "Do not be afraid. Stand firm and you will see the deliverance the LORD will bring you today. The Egyptians you see today you will never see again. The LORD will fight for you; you need only to be still."

Journey 2 Victory

Desires

Psalm 37:4-5

Take delight in the LORD, and he will give you the desires of your heart. Commit your way to the LORD; trust in him and he will do this.

Journey 2 Victory

Destination

Matthew 7:13-14

"Enter through the narrow gate. For wide is the gate and broad is the road that leads to destruction, and many enter through it. But small is the gate and narrow the road that leads to life, and only a few find it."

Journey 2 Victory

Diligence

1 Corinthians 15:58

Therefore, my dear brothers and sisters, stand firm. Let nothing move you. Always give yourselves fully to the work of the Lord, because you know that your labor in the Lord is not in vain.

Journey 2 Victory

Discernment

1 Corinthians 2:14

The person without the Spirit does not accept the things that come from the Spirit of God but considers them foolishness, and cannot understand them because they are discerned only through the Spirit.

Journey 2 Victory

Diligence

1 Corinthians 15:58

Therefore, my dear brothers and sisters, stand firm. Let nothing move you. Always give yourselves fully to the work of the Lord, because you know that your labor in the Lord is not in vain.

Journey 2 Victory

Discernment

1 Corinthians 2:14

The person without the Spirit does not accept the things that come from the Spirit of God but considers them foolishness, and cannot understand them because they are discerned only through the Spirit.

Journey 2 Victory

Discipleship

Matthew 16:24-25

Then Jesus said to his disciples, "Whoever wants to be my disciple must deny themselves and take up their cross and follow me. For whoever wants to save their life will lose it, but whoever loses their life for me will find it."

Discourage

2 Chronicles 20:15

He said: "Listen, King Jehoshaphat and all who live in Judah and Jerusalem! This is what the LORD says to you: 'Do not be afraid or discouraged because of this vast army. For the battle is not yours, but God's."

Journey 2 Victory

Discover

2 Corinthians 11:13-15

For such people are false apostles, deceitful workers, masquerading as apostles of Christ. And no wonder, for Satan himself masquerades as an angel of light. It is not surprising, then, if his servants also masquerade as servants of righteousness. Their end will be what their actions deserve.

Journey 2 Victory

Disposition

John 3:6

Flesh gives birth to flesh, but the Spirit gives birth to spirit.

Journey 2 Victory

Distribution

John 3:8

"The wind blows wherever it pleases. You hear its sound, but you cannot tell where it comes from or where it is going. So it is with everyone born of the Spirit."

Journey 2 Victory

Doubt

Luke 24:38-39

He said to them, "Why are you troubled, and why do doubts rise in your minds? Look at my hands and my feet. It is I myself! Touch me and see; a ghost does not have flesh and bones, as you see I have."

Journey 2 Victory

Dream

Ecclesiastes 5:7

Much dreaming and many words are meaningless. Therefore fear God.

Dryness

Psalm 1:1-3

Blessed is the one who does not walk in step with the wicked or stand in the way that sinners take or sit in the company of mockers, but whose delight is in the law of the LORD, and who meditates on his law day and night. That person is like a tree planted by streams of water, which yields its fruit in season and whose leaf does not wither—whatever they do prosper.

Journey 2 Victory

Duty

Ecclesiastes 12:13-14

Now all has been heard; here is the conclusion of the matter: Fear God and keep his commandment, for this is the duty of all mankind. For God will bring every deed into judgment, including every hidden thing, whether it is good or evil.

Journey 2 Victory

Dynamic

Genesis 5:3

When Adam had lived 130 years, he had a son in his own likeness, in his own image named him Seth.

Edge

Song of Solomon 2:15

Catch for us the foxes, the little foxes that ruin the vineyards, and our vineyards that are in bloom.

Journey 2 Victory

Edify

1 Corinthians 14:33

For God is not a God of disorder but of peace—as in all the congregations of the Lord's people.

Journey 2 Victory

Efficiency

Genesis 1:2

Now the earth was formless and empty, darkness was over the surface of the deep, and the Spirit of God was hovering over the waters.

Effort

2 Samuel 22:38-40

"I pursued my enemies and crushed them; I did not turn back till they were destroyed. I crushed them completely, and they could not rise; they fell beneath my feet. You armed me with strength for battle; you before me."

Journey 2 Victory

Ego

Philippians 2:4-6

Now this is what the LORD Almighty says: "Give careful thought to your ways. You have planted much, but harvested little. You eat, but never have enough. You drink, but never have your fill. You put on clothes, but are not warm. You earn wages, only to put them in a purse with holes in

Journey 2 Victory

Emerging

1 Timothy 3:2

Now the overseer is to be above reproach, faithful to his wife, temperate, self-controlled, respectable, hospitable, able to teach,

Journey 2 Victory

Emotions

Proverbs 15:18

A hot-tempered person stirs up conflict, but the one who is patient calms a quarrel.

Journey 2 Victory

Empowered

Isaiah 61:1

The Spirit of the Sovereign LORD is on me, because the LORD has anointed me to proclaim good news to the poor. He has sent me to bind up the brokenhearted, to proclaim freedom for the captives and release from darkness for the prisoners,

Journey 2 Victory

Emptiness

Matthew 11:28-29

"Come to me, all you who are weary and burdened, and I will give you rest. Take my yoke upon you and learn from me, for I am gentle and humble in heart, and you will find rest for your souls."

Journey 2 Victory

Encourage

Hebrews 3:13

But encourage one another daily, as long as it is called "Today," so that none of you may be hardened by sin's deceitfulness.

Journey 2 Victory

Encouragement

Mark 11:24

Therefore I tell you, whatever you ask for in prayer, believe that you have received it, and it will be yours.

Journey 2 Victory

Endurance

James 1:2

Blessed is the one who perseveres under trial because, having stood the test, that person will receive the crown of life that the Lord has promised to those who love him.

Journey 2 Victory

Enemies

Proverbs 16:7

When the LORD takes pleasure in anyone's way, he causes their enemies to make peace with them.

Journey 2 Victory

Enrich

1 John 2:27

As for you, the anointing you received from him remains in you, and you do not need anyone to teach you. But as his anointing teaches you about all things and as that anointing is real, not counterfeit—just as it has taught you, remain in him.

Journey 2 Victory

Envision

Acts 2:38

Peter replied, "Repent and be baptized, every one of you, in the name of Jesus Christ for the forgiveness of your sins. And you will receive the gift of the Holy Spirit."

Evolve

Revelation 21:3-4

And I heard a loud voice from the throne saying, "Look! God's dwelling place is now among the people and he will dwell with them. They will be his people, and God himself will be with them and be their God. 'He will wipe every tear from their eyes. There will be no more death or mourning or crying or pain, for the old order of things has passed away."

Example

2 Thessalonians 3:9

We did this, not because we do not have the right to such help, but in order to offer ourselves as a model for you to imitate.

Journey 2 Victory

Excuses

Judges 6:15-16

"Pardon me, my lord," Gideon replied, "but how can I save Israel? My clan is the weakest in Manasseh, and I am the least in my family."

The LORD answered, "I will be with you, and you will strike down all the Midianites, leaving none alive."

Journey 2 Victory

Execute

Deuteronomy 28:47-48

Because you did not serve the LORD your God joyfully and gladly in the time of prosperity, therefore in hunger and thirst, in nakedness and dire poverty, you will serve the enemies the LORD sends against you. He will put an iron yoke on your neck until he has destroyed you.

Journey 2 Victory

Expectation

2 Corinthians 8:5

And they exceeded our expectations: They gave themselves first of all to the Lord, and then by the will of God also to us.

Journey 2 Victory

Experience

Acts 2:17-18

" 'In the last days, God says, I will pour out my Spirit on all people. Your sons and daughters will prophesy, your young men will see visions; your old men will dream dreams. Even on my servants, both men and women, I will pour out my Spirit in those days, and they will prophesy."

Journey 2 Victory

Failure

Proverbs 28:13

Whoever conceals their sins does not prosper, but the one who confesses and renounces them finds mercy.

Fairness

James 2:1

My brothers and sisters, believers in our glorious Lord Jesus Christ must not show favoritism.

Journey 2 Victory

Faith

Matthew 21:21-22

Jesus replied, "Truly I tell you, if you have faith and do not doubt, not only can you do what was done to the fig tree, but also you can say to this mountain, 'Go, throw yourself into the sea,' and it will be done. If you believe, you will receive whatever you ask for in prayer."

Journey 2 Victory

Faithfulness

1 Corinthians 10:13

No temptation has overtaken you except what is common to mankind. And God is faithful; he will not let you be tempted beyond what you can bear. But when you are tempted, he will also provide a way out so that you can endure it.

Journey 2 Victory

Family

Malachi 2:16

*"The man who hates and divorces his wife," says the L*ORD*, the God of Israel, "does violence to the one he should protect," says the L*ORD *Almighty.*

So be on your guard, and do not be unfaithful.

Journey 2 Victory

Fantastic

Hebrews 4:16

Let us then approach God's throne of grace with confidence, so that we may receive mercy and find grace to help us in our time of need.

Fatigue

Isaiah 40:29-31

*He gives strength to the weary and increases the power of the weak. Even youths grow tired and weary, and young men stumble and fall; but those who hope in the L*ORD *will renew their strength. They will soar on wings like eagles; they will run and not grow weary, they will walk and not be faint.*

Journey 2 Victory

Favor

Luke 2:52

And Jesus grew in wisdom and stature, and in favor with God and man.

Journey 2 Victory

Flexibility

2 Timothy 2:15

Do your best to present yourself to God as one approved, a worker who does not need to be ashamed and who correctly handles the word of truth.

Journey 2 Victory

Finding

Jeremiah 29:13

You will seek me and find me when you seek me with all your heart.

Finishing

2 Timothy 4:7

I have fought the good fight, I have finished the race, and I have kept the faith.

Journey 2 Victory

Focus

Hebrews 12:2

Fixing our eyes on Jesus, the pioneer and perfecter of faith. For the joy set before him he endured the cross, scorning its shame, and sat down at the right hand of the throne of God.

Journey 2 Victory

Foolish

1 Corinthians 1:27

But God chose the foolish things of the world to shame the wise; God chose the weak things of the world to shame the strong.

Journey 2 Victory

Forgiveness

Matthew 6:14-15

For if you forgive other people when they sin against you, your heavenly Father will also forgive you. But if you do not forgive others their sins, your Father will not forgive your sins.

Journey 2 Victory

Freedom

Genesis 2:15-17

The LORD God took the man and put him in the Garden of Eden to work it and take care of it. And the LORD God commanded the man, "You are free to eat from any tree in the garden; but you must not eat from the tree of the knowledge of good and evil, for when you eat from it you will.

Journey 2 Victory

Friendship

Ecclesiastes 4:9-12

Two are better than one, because they have a good return for their labor: If either of them falls down, one can help the other up. But pity anyone who falls and has no one to help them up. Also, if two lie down together, they will keep warm. But how can one keep warm alone? Though one may be overpowered, two can defend themselves. A cord of three strands is not quickly broken.

Frustration

1 Peter 5:7

Cast all your anxiety on him because he cares for you.

Journey 2 Victory

Fun

Proverbs 5:18-19

May your fountain be blessed, and may you rejoice in the wife of your youth. A loving doe, a graceful deer—may her breasts satisfy you always, may you ever be intoxicated with her love.

Journey 2 Victory

Fundamentals

Acts 2:38

Peter replied, "Repent and be baptized, every one of you, in the name of Jesus Christ for the forgiveness of your sins. And you will receive the gift Spirit.

Journey 2 Victory

Future

Proverbs 16:9

In their hearts humans plan their course, but the LORD establishes their steps.

Journey 2 Victory

Generations

Genesis 17:7

I will establish my covenant as an everlasting covenant between me and you and your descendants after you for the generations to come, to be your God and the God of your descendants after you.

Journey 2 Victory

Generosity

2 Corinthians 9:6

Remember this: Whoever sows sparingly will also reap sparingly, and whoever sows generously will also reap generously.

Gentleness

1 Peter 3:15

But in your hearts revere Christ as Lord. Always be prepared to give an answer to everyone who asks you to give the reason for the hope that you have. But do this with gentleness and respect.

Journey 2 Victory

Gifts

Ephesians 2:8-9

For it is by grace you have been saved, through faith—and this is not from yourselves, it is the gift of God—not by works, so that no one can boast.

Give Up

Acts 20:35

"In everything I did, I showed you that by this kind of hard work we must help the weak, remembering the words the Lord Jesus himself said: 'It is more blessed to give than to receive.'"

Goal

1 Timothy 1:5

The goal of this command is love, which comes from a pure heart and a good conscience and a sincere faith.

Journey 2 Victory

Good-bye

Luke 9:61-62

Still another said, "I will follow you, Lord; but first let me go back and say goodbye to my family." Jesus replied, "No one who puts a hand to the plow and looks back is fit for service in the kingdom of God."

Journey 2 Victory

Goodness

2 Peter 1:5

For this very reason, make every effort to add to your faith goodness; and to goodness, knowledge;

Grace

Isaiah 26:10

But when grace is shown to the wicked, they do not learn righteousness; even in a land of uprightness they go on doing evil and do not regard the majesty of the LORD.

Journey 2 Victory

Gratitude

Colossians 3:16

Let the message of Christ dwell among you richly as you teach and admonish one another with all wisdom through Psalms, hymns, and songs from the Spirit, singing to God with gratitude in your hearts.

Journey 2 Victory

Greatness

1 Chronicles 29:11

Yours, LORD, is the greatness and the power and the glory and the majesty and the splendor, for everything in heaven and earth is yours. Yours, LORD, is the kingdom; you are exalted as head over all.

Journey 2 Victory

Grief

Ecclesiastes 1:18

For with much wisdom comes much sorrow; the more knowledge, the more grief.

Journey 2 Victory

Guard Your Heart

Proverbs 4:23

Above all else, guard your heart, for everything you do flows from it.

Journey 2 Victory

Guidance

Proverbs 11:14

For lack of guidance a nation falls, but victory is won through many advisers.

Guilt

Deuteronomy 5:11

"You shall not misuse the name of the LORD your God, for the LORD will not hold anyone guiltless who misuses his name."

Journey 2 Victory

Gumption

Luke 2:40

And the child grew and became strong; he was filled with wisdom, and the grace of God was on him.

Journey 2 Victory

Habits

Galatians 5:19-21

The acts of the flesh are obvious: sexual immorality, impurity and debauchery; idolatry and witchcraft; hatred, discord, jealousy, fits of rage, selfish ambition, dissensions, factions and envy; drunkenness, orgies, and the like. I warn you, as I did before, that those who live like this will not inherit the kingdom of God.

Journey 2 Victory

Happiness

Ecclesiastes 2:26

To the person who pleases him, God gives wisdom, knowledge and happiness, but to the sinner he gives the task of gathering and storing up wealth to hand it over to the one who pleases God. This too is meaningless, a chasing after the wind.

Journey 2 Victory

Hard work

2 Thessalonians 3:10-12

For even when we were with you, we gave you this rule: "The one who is unwilling to work shall not eat."

We hear that some among you are idle and disruptive. They are not busy; they are busybodies. Such people we command and urge in the Lord Jesus Christ to settle down and earn the food they eat.

Journey 2 Victory

Harmony

Romans 12:16

Live in harmony with one another. Do not be proud, but be willing to associate with people of low position. Do not be conceited.

Journey 2 Victory

Healing

Matthew 9:35

Jesus went through all the towns and villages, teaching in their synagogues, proclaiming the good news of the kingdom and healing every disease and sickness.

Healthy

Luke 11:34

Your eye is the lamp of your body. When your eyes are healthy, your whole body also is full of light. But when they are unhealthy, your body also is full of darkness.

Journey 2 Victory

Heaven

Revelation 21:1-3

Then I saw "a new heaven and a new earth, "for the first heaven and the first earth had passed away, and there was no longer any sea. I saw the Holy City, the new Jerusalem, coming down out of heaven from God, prepared as a bride beautifully dressed for her husband. And I heard a loud voice from the throne saying, "Look! God's dwelling place is now among the people and he will dwell with them. They will be his people, and God himself will be with them and be their God."

Journey 2 Victory

Heritage

1 Peter 1:3-4

Praise be to the God and Father of our Lord Jesus Christ! In his great mercy he has given us new birth into a living hope through the resurrection of Jesus Christ from the dead, and into an inheritance that can never perish, spoil or fade. This inheritance is kept in heaven for you,

Holiness

Ezekiel 38:23

And so I will show my greatness and my holiness, and I will make myself known in the sight of many nations. Then they will know that I am the LORD.

Journey 2 Victory

Honor

Hebrews 13:4

Marriage should be honored by all, and the marriage bed kept pure, for God will judge the adulterer and all the sexually immoral.

Journey 2 Victory

Hope

1 John 3:3

All who have this hope in him purify themselves, just as he is pure.

Journey 2 Victory

Humility

1 Peter 5:5

In the same way, you who are younger, submit yourselves to your elders. All of you, clothe yourselves with humility toward one another, because, "God opposes the proud but shows favor to the humble."

Humor

Proverbs 17:22

A cheerful heart is good medicine, but a crushed spirit dries up the bones.

Journey 2 Victory

Hungry

Isaiah 58:10

And if you spend yourselves in behalf of the hungry and satisfy the needs of the oppressed, then your light will rise in the darkness, and your night will become like the noonday.

Journey 2 Victory

Idolatry

Colossians 3:5

Put to death, therefore, whatever belongs to your earthly nature: sexual immorality, impurity, lust, evil desires and greed, which is idolatry.

Journey 2 Victory

Ignite

1 Corinthians 14:3

But the one who prophesies speaks to people for their strengthening, and comfort.

Imagination

Ephesians 1:17-18

I keep asking that the God of our Lord Jesus Christ, the glorious Father, may give you the Spirit of wisdom and revelation, so that you may know him better. I pray that the eyes of your heart may be enlightened in order that you may know the hope to which he has called you, the riches of his glorious inheritance in his holy people,

Journey 2 Victory

Impact

1 Peter 3:1

Wives, in the same way submit yourselves to your own husbands so that, if any of them do not believe the word, they may be won over without words by the behavior of their wives,

Journey 2 Victory

Impatient

Proverbs 19:2-3

Desire without knowledge is not good—how much more will hasty feet miss the way! A person's own folly leads to their ruin, yet their heart rages against the LORD.

Journey 2 Victory

Incredible

Acts 26:8

Why should any of you consider it incredible that God raises the dead?

Journey 2 Victory

Independence

James 4:7-8

Submit yourselves, then, to God. Resist the devil, and he will flee from you. Come near to God and he will come near to you. Wash your hands, you sinners, and purify your hearts, you double-minded.

Journey 2 Victory

Injustice

Exodus 22:22

"Do not take advantage of the widow or the fatherless. "

Journey 2 Victory

Insight

2 Timothy 2:7

Reflect on what I am saying, for the Lord will give you insight into all this.

Journey 2 Victory

Integrity

Proverbs 10:9

Whoever walks in integrity walks securely, but whoever takes crooked paths will be found out.

Intentional

James 5:12

Above all, my brothers and sisters, do not swear—not by heaven or by earth or by anything else. All you need to say is a simple "Yes" or "No." Otherwise you will be condemned.

Journey 2 Victory

Intimacy

1 Corinthians 7:2-7

But since sexual immorality is occurring, each man should have sexual relations with his own wife, and each woman with her own husband. The husband should fulfill his marital duty to his wife, and likewise the wife to her husband. The wife does not have authority over her own body but yields it to her husband. In the same way, the husband does not have authority over his own body but yields it to his wife. Do not deprive each other except perhaps by mutual consent and for a time, so that you may devote yourselves to prayer. Then come together again so that Satan will not tempt you because of your lack of self-control. I say this as a concession, not as a command. I wish that all of you were as I am. But each of you has your own gift from God; one has this gift, another has that.

Intuition

Ephesians 1:17

I keep asking that the God of our Lord Jesus Christ, the glorious Father, may give you the Spirit of wisdom and revelation, so that you may know him better.

Investment

Luke 6:38

"Give, and it will be given to you. A good measure, pressed down, shaken together and running over, will be poured into your lap. For with the measure you use, it will be measured to you."

Joy

Job 8:21

He will yet fill your mouth with laughter and your lips with shouts of joy.

Journey 2 Victory

Justice

Isaiah 56:1

*This is what the LORD says:
"Maintain justice and do what is right, for my salvation is close at hand and my righteousness will soon be revealed."*

Journey 2 Victory

Kindness

Galatians 6:10

Therefore, as we have opportunity, let us do good to all people, especially to those who belong to the family of believers.

Journey 2 Victory

Leadership

Acts 1:20

"For," said Peter, "it is written in the Book of Psalms: " 'May his place be deserted; let there be no one to dwell in it,' and, " 'May another take his place of leadership.' "

Journey 2 Victory

Learn

Matthew 11:29

Take my yoke upon you and learn from me, for I am gentle and humble in heart, and you will find rest for your souls.

Journey 2 Victory

Liaison

1 Timothy 3:2

Now the overseer is to be above reproach, faithful to his wife, temperate, self-controlled, respectable, hospitable, and able to teach.

Journey 2 Victory

Lighthouse

John 8:12

"When Jesus spoke again to the people, he said, "I am the light of the world. Whoever follows me will never walk in darkness, but will have the light of life."

Journey 2 Victory

Limitations

Romans 6:19

I am using an example from everyday life because of your human limitations. Just as you used to offer yourselves as slaves to impurity and to ever-increasing wickedness, so now offer yourselves as slaves to righteousness leading to holiness.

Journey 2 Victory

Listening

Proverbs 19:20

Listen to advice and accept discipline, and at the end you will be counted among the wise.

Journey 2 Victory

Loneliness

Isaiah 41:10

So do not fear, for I am with you; do not be dismayed, for I am your God. I will strengthen you and help you; I will uphold you with my righteous right hand.

Love

2 Timothy 2:22

Flee the evil desires of youth and pursue righteousness, faith, love and peace, along with those who call on the Lord out of a pure heart.

Journey 2 Victory

Loyalty

Titus 3:1

Remind the people to be subject to rulers and authorities, to be obedient; to be ready to do whatever is good,

Journey 2 Victory

Maintenance

Deuteronomy 20:5

Then the officers shall speak to the people, saying, 'Is there any man who has built a new house and has not dedicated it? Let him go back to his house, lest he die in the battle and another man dedicate it.

Manners

Ephesians 4:29

Do not let any unwholesome talk come out of your mouths, but only what is helpful for building others up according to their needs, that it may benefit those who listen.

Journey 2 Victory

Mastering

Hebrews 13:4

Marriage should be honored by all, and the marriage bed kept pure, for God will judge the adulterer and all the sexually immoral.

Journey 2 Victory

Maturity

1 Corinthians 10:13

No temptation has overtaken you except what is common to mankind. And God is faithful; he will not let you be tempted beyond what you can bear. But when you are tempted, he will also provide a way out so that you can endure it.

Journey 2 Victory

Maximum

Psalm 90:10

Our days may come to seventy years, or eighty, if our strength endures; yet the best of them are but trouble and sorrow, for they quickly pass, and we fly away.

Journey 2 Victory

Meaning

Isaiah 43:7

"Everyone who is called by my name, whom I created for my glory, whom I formed and made."

Mentorship

Psalm 119:103

How sweet are your words to my taste, sweeter than honey to my mouth!

Journey 2 Victory

Mercy

Matthew 9:13

"But go and learn what this means: 'I desire mercy, not sacrifice.' For I have not come to call the righteous, but sinners."

Method

Ephesians 6:4

Fathers, do not exasperate your children; instead, bring them up in the training and instruction of the Lord.

Journey 2 Victory

Ministry

Ephesians 4:11-13

So Christ himself gave the apostles, the prophets, the evangelists, the pastors and teachers, to equip his people for works of service, so that the body of Christ may be built up until we all reach unity in the faith and in the knowledge of the Son of God and become mature, attaining to the whole measure of the fullness of Christ.

Journey 2 Victory

Miracles

Matthew 17:20

He replied, "Because you have so little faith. Truly I tell you, if you have faith as small as a mustard seed, you can say to this mountain, 'Move from here to there,' and it will move. Nothing will be impossible for you."

Journey 2 Victory

Mistakes

1 John 1:9

If we confess our sins, he is faithful and just and will forgive us our sins and purify us from all unrighteousness.

Money

Matthew 6:24

"No one can serve two masters. Either you will hate the one and love the other, or you will be devoted to the one and despise the other. You cannot serve both God and money."

Journey 2 Victory

Motivation

1 Corinthians 15:58

Therefore, my dear brothers and sisters, stand firm. Let nothing move you. Always give yourselves fully to the work of the Lord, because you know that your labor in the Lord is not in vain.

Journey 2 Victory

Motives

Proverbs 21:2

A person may think their own ways are right, but the LORD weighs the heart.

Journey 2 Victory

Multiplication

Matthew 4:4

Jesus answered, "It is written: 'Man shall not live on bread alone, but on every word that comes from the mouth of God.'"

Naïve

Romans 16:18

For such people are not serving our Lord Christ, but their own appetites. By smooth talk and flattery they deceive the minds of naive people.

Journey 2 Victory

Nation

1 Timothy 2:1-2

I urge, then, first of all, that petitions, prayers, intercession and thanksgiving be made for all people—for kings and all those in authority, that we may live peaceful and quiet lives in all godliness and holiness.

Journey 2 Victory

Needs

Matthew 6:33-34

But seek first his kingdom and his righteousness, and all these things will be given to you as well. Therefore do not worry about tomorrow, for tomorrow will worry about itself. Each day has enough trouble of its own.

Neighbor

John 13:34-35

"A new command I give you: Love one another. As I have loved you, so you must love one another. By this everyone will know that you are my disciples, if you love one another."

Nurture

1 Thessalonians 5:14-15

And we urge you, brothers and sisters, warn those who are idle and disruptive, encourage the disheartened, help the weak, be patient with everyone. Make sure that nobody pays back wrong for wrong, but always strive to do what is good for each other and for everyone else.

Journey 2 Victory

Obedient

Titus 3:1

Remind the people to be subject to rulers and authorities, to be obedient; to be ready to do whatever is good,

Obligation

Romans 8:12

Therefore, brothers and sisters, we have an obligation—but it is not to the flesh, to live according to it.

Journey 2 Victory

Obstacle

Romans 16:17

I urge you, brothers and sisters, to watch out for those who cause divisions and put obstacles in your way that are contrary to the teaching you have learned. Keep away from them.

Journey 2 Victory

Opportunity

Galatians 6:10

Therefore, as we have opportunity, let us do good to all people, especially to those who belong to the family of believers.

Opposition

Matthew 5:11-12

"Blessed are you when people insult you, persecute you and falsely say all kinds of evil against you because of me. Rejoice and be glad, because great is your reward in heaven, for in the same way they persecuted the prophets who were before you."

Journey 2 Victory

Optimism

Romans 8:28

And we know that in all things God works for the good of those who love him, who have been called according to his purpose.

Journey 2 Victory

Options

John 14:6

Jesus answered, "I am the way and the truth and the life. No one comes to the Father except through me."

Order

1 Corinthians 14:40

But everything should be done in a fitting and orderly way.

Journey 2 Victory

Overcome

John 16:3

"I have told you these things, so that in me you may have peace. In this world you will have trouble. But take heart! I have overcome the world."

Overwhelmed

2 Corinthians 2:7

Now instead, you ought to forgive and comfort him, so that he will not be overwhelmed by excessive sorrow.

Journey 2 Victory

Pain

Revelation 21:4

"He will wipe every tear from their eyes. There will be no more death' or mourning or crying or pain, for the old order of things has passed away."

Journey 2 Victory

Paradigm

Colossians 3:5

Put to death, therefore, whatever belongs to your earthly nature: sexual immorality, impurity, lust, evil desires and greed, which is idolatry.

Journey 2 Victory

Partnership

Philemon 6

I pray that your partnership with us in the faith may be effective in deepening your understanding of every good thing we share for the sake of Christ.

Past

Isaiah 43:18-19

"Forget the former things; do not dwell on the past. See, I am doing a new thing! Now it springs up; do you not perceive it? I am making a way in the wilderness and streams in the wasteland."

Journey 2 Victory

Patience

Proverbs 19:11

A person's wisdom yields patience; it is to one's glory to overlook an offense.

Perception

John 16:13

But when he, the Spirit of truth, comes, he will guide you into all the truth. He will not speak on his own; he will speak only what he hears, and he will tell you what is yet to come.

Journey 2 Victory

Perfect

Matthew 5:48

Be perfect, therefore, as your heavenly Father is perfect.

Personality

1 Samuel 16:7

But the LORD said to Samuel, "Do not consider his appearance or his height, for I have rejected him. The LORD does not look at the things people look at. People look at the outward appearance, but the LORD looks at the heart."

Journey 2 Victory

Perspective

Revelation 21:8

"But the cowardly, the unbelieving, the vile, the murderers, the sexually immoral, those who practice magic arts, the idolaters and all liars—they will be consigned to the fiery lake of burning sulfur. This is the second death."

Pleasure

Psalm 16:11

You make known to me the path of life; you will fill me with joy in your presence, with eternal pleasures at your right hand.

Journey 2 Victory

Plunge

1 Timothy 6:9

Those who want to get rich fall into temptation and a trap and into many foolish and harmful desires that plunge people into ruin and destruction.

Poise

Job 37:16

Do you know how the clouds hang poised, those wonders of him who has perfect knowledge?

Journey 2 Victory

Positivity

Philippians 4:8

Finally, brothers and sisters, whatever is true, whatever is noble, whatever is right, whatever is pure, whatever is lovely, whatever is admirable—if anything is excellent or praiseworthy—think about such things.

Potential

Joshua 1:5

No one will be able to stand against you all the days of your life. As I was with Moses, so I will be with you; I will never leave you nor forsake you.

Journey 2 Victory

Power

2 Timothy 1:7

For the Spirit God gave us does not make us timid, but gives us power, love and self-discipline.

Journey 2 Victory

Prayer

Matthew 6:9-13

"This, then, is how you should pray: "Our Father in heaven, hallowed be your name, your kingdom come, your will be done, on earth as it is in heaven. Give us today our daily bread. And forgive us our debts, as we also have forgiven our debtors. And lead us not into temptation but deliver us from the evil one."

Journey 2 Victory

Precious

Psalm 72:4

He will rescue them from oppression and violence, for precious is their blood in his sight.

Journey 2 Victory

Prepare

Matthew 7:24

"Therefore everyone who hears these words of mine and puts them into practice is like a wise man who built his house on the rock."

Journey 2 Victory

Present

Galatians 2:20

I have been crucified with Christ and I no longer live, but Christ lives in me. The life I now live in the body, I live by faith in the Son of God, who loved me and gave himself for me.

Journey 2 Victory

Pressure

2 Corinthians 11:28

Besides everything else, I face daily the pressure of my concern for all the churches.

Journey 2 Victory

Pride

Proverbs 16:18

Pride goes before destruction, a haughty spirit before a fall.

Journey 2 Victory

Productivity

Luke 6:45

A good man brings good things out of the good stored up in his heart, and an evil man brings evil things out of the evil stored up in his heart. For the mouth speaks what the heart is full of.

Journey 2 Victory

Professional

2 Timothy 3:16-17

All Scripture is God-breathed and is useful for teaching, rebuking, correcting and training in righteousness, so that the servant of God may be thoroughly equipped for every good work.

Journey 2 Victory

Projection

Leviticus 20:6

"'Do not turn to mediums or seek out spiritists, for you will be defiled by them. I am the LORD your God.'"

Journey 2 Victory

Promise

2 Peter 3:9

The Lord is not slow in keeping his promise, as some understand slowness. Instead he is patient with you, not wanting anyone to perish, but everyone to come to repentance.

Journey 2 Victory

Prompt

Job 15:5

Your sin prompts your mouth; you adopt the tongue of the crafty.

Journey 2 Victory

Purity

1 Timothy 4:12

Don't let anyone look down on you because you are young, but set an example for the believers in speech, in conduct, in love, in faith and in purity.

Purpose

Exodus 9:16

But I have raised you up for this very purpose, that I might show you my power and that my name might be proclaimed in all the earth.

Pursue

Psalm 57:3

He sends from heaven and saves me, rebuking those who hotly pursue me—God sends forth his love and his faithfulness.

Quality

Leviticus 27:14

"'If anyone dedicates their house as something holy to the LORD, the priest will judge its quality as good or bad. Whatever value the priest then sets, so it will remain.'"

Quitting

Galatians 6:9

Let us not become weary in doing good, for at the proper time we will reap a harvest if we do not give up.

Journey 2 Victory

Reconciliation

2 Corinthians 5:18

All this is from God, who reconciled us to himself through Christ and gave us the ministry of reconciliation.

Journey 2 Victory

Reflect

Proverbs 27:19

As water reflects the face, so one's life reflects the heart.

Journey 2 Victory

Rejection

Romans 11:5

For if their rejection brought reconciliation to the world, what will their acceptance be life from the dead?

Journey 2 Victory

Relationship

Philippians 2:5

In your relationships with one another, have the same mindset as Christ Jesus.

Relevance

Leviticus 20:22-23

'Keep all my decrees and laws and follow them, so that the land where I am bringing you to live may not vomit you out. You must not live according to the customs of the nations I am going to drive out before you. Because they did all these things, I abhorred them.'

Journey 2 Victory

Remarriage

Matthew 5:31-32

"It has been said, 'Anyone who divorces his wife must give her a certificate of divorce.' But I tell you that anyone who divorces his wife, except for sexual immorality, makes her the victim of adultery, and anyone who marries a divorced woman commits adultery."

Journey 2 Victory

Renewal

2 Corinthians 4:16

Therefore we do not lose heart. Though outwardly we are wasting away, yet inwardly we are being renewed day by day.

Journey 2 Victory

Reputation

1 Timothy 3:7

He must also have a good reputation with outsiders, so that he will not fall into disgrace and into the devil's trap.

Resist

James 4:7

Submit yourselves, then, to God. Resist the devil, and he will flee from you.

Journey 2 Victory

Resolution

2 Timothy 2:15

Do your best to present yourself to God as one approved, a worker who does not need to be ashamed and who correctly handles the word of truth.

Journey 2 Victory

Respect

1 Peter 2:17

Show proper respect to everyone, love the family of believers, fear God, and honor the emperor.

Journey 2 Victory

Responsibility

1 Timothy 5:8

Anyone who does not provide for their relatives, and especially for their own household, has denied the faith and is worse than an unbeliever.

Rest

Matthew 11:28

"Come to me, all you who are weary and burdened, and I will give you rest."

Journey 2 Victory

Restlessness

James 3:8

But no human being can tame the tongue. It is a restless evil, full of deadly poison.

Journey 2 Victory

Restore

Job 22:23

If you return to the Almighty, you will be restored: if you remove wickedness far from your tent.

Journey 2 Victory

Result

Ezra 9:13

"What has happened to us is a result of our evil deeds and our great guilt, and yet, our God, you have punished us less than our sins deserved and have given us a remnant like this."

Journey 2 Victory

Retention

Psalm 32:8

I will instruct you and teach you in the way you should go; I will counsel you with my loving eye on you.

Journey 2 Victory

Revenge

Romans 12:19

Do not take revenge, my dear friends, but leave room for God's wrath, for it is written: "It is mine to avenge; I will repay," says the Lord.

Risk

2 Samuel 23:17

"Far be it from me, LORD, to do this!" he said. "Is it not the blood of men who went at the risk of their lives?" And David would not drink it. Such were the exploits of the three mighty warriors.

Journey 2 Victory

Roles

1 Corinthians 3:16

Don't you know that you yourselves are God's temple and that God's Spirit dwells in your midst?

Romance

Proverbs 5:18-19

May your fountain be blessed, and may you rejoice in the wife of your youth. A loving doe, a graceful deer—may her breasts satisfy you always, may you ever be intoxicated with her love.

Journey 2 Victory

Sacrifice

Hebrews 13:16

And do not forget to do good and to share with others, for with such sacrifices God is pleased.

Salvation

Exodus 15:2

"The LORD is my strength and my defense; he has become my salvation. He is my God, and I will praise him, my father's God, and I will exalt him."

Sanity

James 1:5

If any of you lacks wisdom, you should ask God, who gives generously to all without finding fault, and it will be given to you.

Satisfaction

Ecclesiastes 2:24

A person can do nothing better than to eat and drink and find satisfaction in their own toil. This too, I see, is from the hand of God.

Journey 2 Victory

Schedule

Ecclesiastes 9:10

Whatever your hand finds to do, do it with all your might, for in the realm of the dead, where you are going, there is neither working nor planning nor knowledge nor wisdom.

Scope

John 1:14

The Word became flesh and made his dwelling among us. We have seen his glory, the glory of the one and only Son, who came from the Father, full of grace and truth.

Journey 2 Victory

Security

Proverbs 22:26

Do not be one who shakes hands in pledge or puts up security for debts.

Seduction

Romans 6:12-13

Therefore do not let sin reign in your mortal body so that you obey its evil desires. Do not offer any part of yourself to sin as an instrument of wickedness, but rather offer yourselves to God as those who have been brought from death to life; and offer every part of yourself to him as an instrument of righteousness.

Journey 2 Victory

Servant

Isaiah 61:1-2

The Spirit of the Sovereign LORD is on me, because the LORD has anointed me to proclaim good news to the poor. He has sent me to bind up the brokenhearted, to proclaim freedom for the captives and release from darkness for the prisoners to proclaim the year of the LORD's favor and the day of vengeance of our God, to comfort all who mourn.

Journey 2 Victory

Sharing

Philippians 2:1

Therefore if you have any encouragement from being united with Christ, if any comfort from his love, if any common sharing in the Spirit, if any tenderness and compassion,

Journey 2 Victory

Simple

Proverbs 8:5

You who are simple, gain prudence; you who are foolish, set your hearts on it.

Skeptic

Acts 10:34

Then Peter began to speak: "I now realize how true it is that God does not show favoritism"

Journey 2 Victory

Solitude

Matthew 6:6

But when you pray, go into your room, close the door and pray to your Father, who is unseen. Then your Father, who sees what is done in secret, will reward you.

Sorrow

2 Corinthians 7:10

Godly sorrow brings repentance that leads to salvation and leaves no regret, but worldly sorrow brings death.

Journey 2 Victory

Stability

Isaiah 33:6

He will be the sure foundation for your times, a rich store of salvation and wisdom and knowledge; the fear of the LORD is the key to this treasure.

Status

James 1:26

Those who consider themselves religious and yet do not keep a tight rein on their tongues deceive themselves, and their religion is worthless.

Journey 2 Victory

Steadfast

1 Peter 5:10

And the God of all grace, who called you to his eternal glory in Christ, after you have suffered a little while, will himself restore you and make you strong, firm and steadfast.

Storm

Nahum 1:3

The LORD is slow to anger but great in power; the LORD will not leave the guilty unpunished. His way is in the whirlwind and the storm, and clouds are the dust of his feet.

Strength

Exodus 15:2

"The LORD is my strength and my defense; he has become my salvation. He is my God, and I will praise him, my father's God, and I will exalt him."

Journey 2 Victory

Stress

Titus 3:8

This is a trustworthy saying. And I want you to stress these things, so that those who have trusted in God may be careful to devote themselves to doing what is good. These things are excellent and profitable for everyone.

Stretch

Luke 6:10

He looked around at them all, and then said to the man, "Stretch out your hand." He did so, and his hand was restored.

Strive

Luke 13:24

"Make every effort to enter through the narrow door, because many, I tell you, will try to enter and will not be able to."

Stubborn

Jeremiah 16:12

But you have behaved more wickedly than your ancestors. See how all of you are following the stubbornness of your evil hearts instead of obeying me.

Journey 2 Victory

Success

Joshua 1:8

Keep this Book of the Law always on your lips; meditate on it day and night, so that you may be careful to do everything written in it. Then you will be prosperous and successful.

Journey 2 Victory

Support

Ezra 10:4

"Rise up; this matter is in your hands. We will support you, so take courage and do it."

Surrender

Matthew 16:15

For whoever wants to save their life will lose it, but whoever loses their life for me will find it.

Journey 2 Victory

Symbol

Deuteronomy 11:18

Fix these words of mine in your hearts and minds; tie them as symbols on your hands and bind them on your foreheads.

System

Acts 20:35

"In everything I did, I showed you that by this kind of hard work we must help the weak, remembering the words the Lord Jesus himself said: 'It is more blessed to give than to receive.'"

Journey 2 Victory

Tactical

Psalm 82:4

Rescue the weak and the needy; deliver them from the hand of the wicked.

Talent

Matthew 25:14-30

"Again, it will be like a man going on a journey, who called his servants and entrusted his wealth to them. To one he gave five bags of gold, to another two bags, and to another one bag, each according to his ability. Then he went on his journey. The man who had received five bags of gold went at once and put his money to work and gained five bags more..."

Journey 2 Victory

Teach

2 Timothy 3:16

All Scripture is God-breathed and is useful for teaching, rebuking, correcting and training in righteousness,

Journey 2 Victory

Teamwork

Ecclesiastes 4:9-12

Two are better than one, because they have a good return for their labor: If either of them falls down, one can help the other up. But pity anyone who falls and has no one to help them up. Also, if two lie down together, they will keep warm. But how can one keep warm alone? Though one may be overpowered, two can defend themselves. A cord of three strands is not quickly broken.

Journey 2 Victory

Temptation

1 Corinthians 10:13

No temptation has overtaken you except what is common to mankind. And God is faithful; he will not let you be tempted beyond what you can bear. But when you are tempted, he will also provide a way out so that you can endure it.

Testing

Deuteronomy 13:3

You must not listen to the words of that prophet or dreamer. The LORD your God is testing you to find out whether you love him with all your heart and with all your soul.

Journey 2 Victory

Therapeutic

1 Corinthians 6:18

Flee from sexual immorality. All other sins a person commits are outside the body, but whoever sins sexually, sins against their own body.

Think

Philippians 4:8

Finally, brothers and sisters, whatever is true, whatever is noble, whatever is right, whatever is pure, whatever is lovely, whatever is admirable—if anything is excellent or praiseworthy—think about such things.

Journey 2 Victory

Thoughts

Mark 7:20

He went on: "What comes out of a person is what defiles them."

Journey 2 Victory

Time

Ecclesiastes 3

There is a time for everything, and a season for every activity under the heavens:...

Journey 2 Victory

Timing

Romans 5:6

You see, at just the right time, when we were still powerless, Christ died for the ungodly.

Tithing

Malachi 3:10

Bring the whole tithe into the storehouse, that there may be food in my house. Test me in this, "says the LORD Almighty, "and see if I will not throw open the floodgates of heaven and pour out so much blessing that there will not be room enough to store it.

Journey 2 Victory

Today

Luke 23:43

Jesus answered him, "Truly I tell you, today you will be with me in paradise."

Journey 2 Victory

Training

1 Timothy 4:8

For physical training is of some value, but godliness has value for all things, holding promise for both the present life and the life to come.

Journey 2 Victory

Transgressions

Isaiah 53:5

But he was pierced for our transgressions, he was crushed for our iniquities; the punishment that brought us peace was on him, and by his wounds we are healed.

Tranquility

Ecclesiastes 4:6

Better one handful with tranquility than two handfuls with toil and chasing after the wind.

Journey 2 Victory

Transformation

Romans 12:2

Do not conform to the pattern of this world, but be transformed by the renewing of your mind. Then you will be able to test and approve what God's will is—his good, pleasing and perfect will.

Journey 2 Victory

Transparent

Revelation 21:21

The twelve gates were twelve pearls, each gate made of a single pearl. The great street of the city was of gold, as pure as transparent glass.

Journey 2 Victory

Travel

Judges 19:17

When he looked and saw the traveler in the city square, the old man asked, "Where are you going? Where did you come from?"

Treasure

Matthew 13:44

"The kingdom of heaven is like treasure hidden in a field. When a man found it, he hid it again, and then in his joy went and sold all he had and bought that field."

Journey 2 Victory

Trend

1 Corinthians 6:9-10

Or do you not know that wrongdoers will not inherit the kingdom of God? Do not be deceived: Neither the sexually immoral nor idolaters nor adulterers nor men who have sex with men nor thieves nor the greedy nor drunkards nor slanderers nor swindlers will inherit the kingdom of God.

Trouble

John 16:33

"I have told you these things, so that in me you may have peace. In this world you will have trouble. But take heart! I have overcome the world."

Trust

Luke 16:10

"Whoever can be trusted with very little can also be trusted with much, and whoever is dishonest with very little will also be dishonest with much."

Journey 2 Victory

Trustworthy

1 Timothy 1:15

Here is a trustworthy saying that deserves full acceptance: Christ Jesus came into the world to save sinners—of whom I am the worst.

Journey 2 Victory

Truth

1 Peter 1:22

Now that you have purified yourselves by obeying the truth so that you have sincere love for each other, love one another from the heart.

Journey 2 Victory

Understanding

Philemon 6

I pray that your partnership with us in the faith may be effective in deepening your understanding of every good thing we share for the sake of Christ.

Journey 2 Victory

Unwavering

John 5:30

By myself I can do nothing; I judge only as I hear, and my judgment is just, for I seek not to please myself but him who sent me.

Journey 2 Victory

Used

Ezekiel 7:20

They took pride in their beautiful jewelry and used it to make their detestable idols. They made it into vile images; therefore I will make it a thing unclean for them.

Journey 2 Victory

Value

Habakkuk 2:18

"Of what value is an idol carved by a craftsman? Or an image that teaches lies? For the one who makes it trusts in his own creation; he makes idols that cannot speak."

Journey 2 Victory

Victory

Judges 12:3

"When I saw that you wouldn't help, I took my life in my hands and crossed over to fight the Ammonites, and the LORD gave me the victory over them. Now why have you come up today to fight me?"

Journey 2 Victory

Vision

Acts 2:17

'In the last days, God says, I will pour out my Spirit on all people. Your sons and daughters will prophesy, your young men will see visions, your old men will dream dreams.'

Voice

Luke 3:22

"And the Holy Spirit descended on him in bodily form like a dove. And a voice came from heaven: "You are my Son, whom I love; with you I am well pleased."

Journey 2 Victory

Vulnerability

Hebrews 4:13

Nothing in all creation is hidden from God's sight. Everything is uncovered and laid bare before the eyes of him to whom we must give account.

Journey 2 Victory

Warrior

Proverbs 16:32

Better a patient person than a warrior, one with self-control than one who takes a city.

Journey 2 Victory

Weakness

1 Corinthians 12:9

But he said to me, "My grace is sufficient for you, for my power is made perfect in weakness." Therefore I will boast all the more gladly about my weaknesses, so that Christ's power may rest on me.

Wealth

Revelation 3:17

You say, 'I am rich; I have acquired wealth and do not need a thing.' But you do not realize that you are wretched, pitiful, poor, blind and naked.

Journey 2 Victory

Winner

Proverbs 13:20

Walk with the wise and become wise, for a companion of fools suffers harm.

Witness

1 Thessalonians 2:10

You are witnesses, and so is God, of how holy, righteous and blameless we were among you who believed.

Words

Mark 4:15

Some people are like seed along the path, where the word is sown. As soon as they hear it, Satan comes and takes away the word that was sown in them.

Work

Galatians 3:2

I would like to learn just one thing from you: Did you receive the Spirit by the works of the law, or by believing what you heard?

Worry

Matthew 6:34

Therefore do not worry about tomorrow, for tomorrow will worry about itself. Each day has enough trouble of its own.

Journey 2 Victory

Worship

2 Kings 17:39

"Rather, worship the LORD your God; it is he who will deliver you from the hand of all your enemies."

Journey 2 Victory

Zeal

Romans 12:11

For I can testify about them that they are zealous for God, but their zeal is not based on knowledge.

About the Authors

Mae and Chuck met in 7th grade, dated in High School, and married in 1969, just prior to Chuck's Vietnam tour.

They began mentoring in home Bible studies and saw how their Christ-centered relationship was "different" from others. Though far from "perfect," their marriage and commitment to Christ demonstrated a peace and happiness that intrigued other couples. This became the opportunity to mentor other couples and to teach them to *work* at their relationship and *grow* their *love* for one another (with Christ) each day.

Chuck and Mae have two adult children, Glynn and Barbara, and seven grandchildren.

Executive Director and Founder of Today's Promise, Inc., Chuck is an ordained minister with more than 15-years in couple and professional life-coaching experience. Chuck is known as a premier marriage, relationship, budget and career coaching mentor throughout the nation—having been recognized by the NY Times, CBS Evening News, and the Harvard School of Business, among others. Chuck holds a Bachelor of Science in Business and Finance from Barry University, graduating cum laude. He was formerly employed by the U.S. Under Secretary of the Treasury in local banks as a loan officer, Junior Vice President, and auditor, this provided unprecedented exposure to the financial industry.

He holds many certifications, including a former Florida State Teaching Certificate as an Occupational Therapist for Secondary Education and a Certified Crown Financial Budget Coach/Counselor. He is a Certified Marriage Mentor for PREPARE/ENRICH marriage preparation, and he coaches those already married. He holds certification as a Seminar Director for PREPARE/ENRICH, providing training to clergy, professional counselors, and mentor couples. He proudly serves as a 15th Judicial Circuit Court Registered Provider for marriage education, qualifying couples for discounted marriage licensure. He is a Master Instructor for START SMART, a premarital training course that teaches specific skills to seriously dating or engaged couples. An instructor for PICK a Partner, also known as *"How to Avoid Marrying a Jerk(ette),"* a class that instructs unmarried individuals in how to best prepare for future committed relationships.

Mae recently retired after serving over 40 years in the local school system. She volunteers at Christ Fellowship Church as well as her former elementary school. She and Chuck will serve together in a Florida-wide ministry providing the marriage component for Florida Men of Integrity.

Herman and Sharron Baily recently invited Chuck and Mae as guests on Christian Television Network's *The Herman and Sharon Show* broadcast across 22 stations nation-wide and around the World.

Chuck co-authored *The Solution for Marriages;* dedicated tips to marriage mentors proven to be successful in helping others build the foundation for life-long, satisfying marriages. *The Solution for Marriages* is in English and German.

Their second book, *The Marriage Journey, A Flight Plan to Your Healthy Marriage,* provides the flight plan for marriages to rely on, not if, but when they face the turbulence experienced by every couple. It contains powerful, faith-based references used by the authors in their own 47 plus years of marriage. *The Marriage Journey: A Flight Plan for Your Healthy Marriage* is available in English and Spanish.

Now, *Journey 2 Victory: A Devotional Journal* serves as a tool to assist in healing not only marriages and relationships, but individuals. Many times when thoughts are committed to paper God gives us comfort and 'releases' our hurt and pain. *Journey 2 Victory: A Devotional Journal* is published in English and Spanish.

Other Works by Chuck & Mae

Available at Amazon.com and the Connect with Us web sites

This unique guide, *The Solution for Marriages: Mentoring a New Generation,* provides a comprehensive reference for everyone looking to mentor a couple through today's complex issues. This book masterfully prepares the marriage mentor by combining timeless biblical wisdom, critical relationship skills, and empowering resources that are the keys to a successful marriage.

You will discover how successful marriage mentors guide couples through the essential areas of marriage, including how to:

- Communicate and Improve Their Conflict Resolution Skills
- Grant Forgiveness and Build a Foundation of Trust
- Understand the Impact Cohabitation has on the Marriage
- Discover God's Purpose for Marriage and Sex
- Break Free from the Grip of Pornography
- Protect Their Marriage

Written by two marriage mentors with over 50 years of combined experience in helping couples experience the marriage God intended, you will find nothing else like it on the market. Their expert guidance has enabled pastors, marriage mentors, and couples to courageously wade through the maze of challenging issues that every couple faces.

Die Lösung für Ehen: Ehe-Mentoring - der Weg zu einer neuen Generation von Ehen (German Edition) Ehen aufbauen, die bestehen bleiben: Heute mehr denn je profitieren Paare von kompetenten und erfahrenen Ehementoren, die ehrlich auf die besonderen Hürden des Ehebundes vorbereiten und verheiratete Paare durch Herausforderungen führen können. Mit einem guten Ehe-Mentoring sind die unerfüllte Ehe bzw. die Scheidung keine Optionen mehr! Dieser einzigartige Ratgeber stellt für all jene ein umfangreiches Nachschlagewerk zur Verfügung, die lernbegeisterte Paare in der Ehe, Verlobungs- und Beziehungsphase als Mentoren begleiten möchten. Auf meisterhafte Art verbindet ***Die Lösung für Ehen*** zeitlose und biblisch fundierte Weisheit mit grundlegenden Beziehungskompetenzen und mit hilfreichen Materialien, die für eine erfolgreiche Ehe entscheidend sind. Lasst Euch von erfolgreichen Ehementoren durch die wesentlichen Themengebiete der Ehe begleiten - zum Beispiel: - Gottes Bestimmung für die Ehe und Seine Sichtweise auf die Rollenverteilung - Kommunikation und Konfliktbewältigung auf Augenhöhe - Schutz der Ehe gegenüber dem Internet, sozialen Medien und "Freunden" - Loslösen von der Macht der Pornografie - Vergebung und Vertrauensaufbau als Fundament - Verstehen der Auswirkung von vorehelichem Zusammenleben auf den Ehebund Internationale Ehe-Experten und -Profis sprechen **"Die Lösung für Ehen"** ihre höchste Empfehlung aus. Erlebt, wie Euer Ehe-Mentoring und Eure eigene Ehe von diesem Buch profitieren!

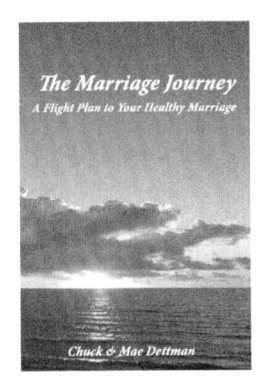

The Marriage Journey, A Flight Plan to Your Healthy Marriage shares skills to create a strong, healthy and lasting marriage. It is designed for couples of any age or stage in their relationship. You can turn a good marriage into a great one, find hope in a struggling one, or take a great marriage to a deeper, more passionate level.

The Marriage Journey gives helpful navigational aids you can easily apply during the stormy times of your marriage flight. The aeronautical theme gives an uplifting perspective to the turbulence often experienced in marriage. ***The Journey*** checkups, flight plans, and more, make for an easy read, plus offer a fresh and unclouded approach to help you build a strong marriage and family.

A successful marriage requires clear flight plans to avoid thunderstorms for a smooth journey. God as the pilot and couples as the co-pilots, couples need to work as a team to make the flight as enjoyable as possible and appreciate the beauty of the skies. The ***Journey*** will help couples have a pleasant trip. Enjoy the flight!

God is the author of the ideal flight plan (the Bible). It is up to the co-pilots (husband and wife) to follow it. If they deviate, they wind up in trouble with the FAA, wander into bad weather, run out of gas, and so on. You have no control over your destiny; it is all in the pilot's hands. God, however, gives us free will so we CAN and DO deviate from His flight plan; He is the big eye in the sky. He is the Air Traffic Controller who can see where the other planes are, and where the storms are, and then vector you around them.

El matrimonio es un viaje: Un de plan de vuelo saludable para tu matrimonio (Spanish Edition) *"**El matrimonio es un viaje**"* provee ayuda útil a la navegación en el matrimonio que usted puede aplicar fácilmente en los momentos tormentosos de su matrimonio. El tema aeronáutico da una perspectiva edificante a la turbulencia experimentada a menudo en su relación. Las revisiones antes del vuelo, planes de viaje, y más, hacen una lectura fácil, además de ofrecer un enfoque fresco y sin nubes para ayudarle a construir un matrimonio y familia sólidos.

Viajar con *"El matrimonio es un viaje"* será inolvidable. Usando la analogía de los viajes en avión, el libro ayuda a las parejas a explorar nuevos territorios y hacer descubrimientos sorprendentes. Un matrimonio exitoso requiere de planes de vuelo claros para evitar las tormentas eléctricas y tener un viaje más satisfactorio. Dios como el piloto y las parejas como los copilotos; las parejas deben trabajar en equipo para hacer que el vuelo sea lo más agradable posible y apreciar la belleza de los cielos. El viaje ayudará a las parejas a tener un viaje placentero. ¡Disfrute del vuelo!

Escrito por el co-autor de *"La solución para los matrimonios"*, *"El matrimonio es un viaje"* comparte habilidades para crear un matrimonio fuerte, saludable y duradero. Está diseñado para parejas de cualquier edad o etapa en su relación. Usted puede convertir un buen matrimonio en uno grandioso, encontrar la esperanza en su lucha por uno, o llevar un gran matrimonio a un nivel profundamente apasionado

Connect with Us

Web: www.todayspromise.org

Web: www.themarriage-journey.com

Twitter: http://twitter.com/MarriageJurney

Facebook: https://www.facebook.com/marriage.journey

Made in the USA
Middletown, DE
13 August 2024